FINGERPICKING
DUKE ELLINGTON

ISBN 978-1-4234-1658-6

Visit Hal Leonard Online at www.halleonard.com

HAL•LEONARD®
CORPORATION
7777 W. BLUEMOUND RD. P.O. BOX 13819 MILWAUKEE, WI 53213

FINGERPICKING
DUKE ELLINGTON

INTRODUCTION TO FINGERSTYLE GUITAR

Fingerstyle (a.k.a. fingerpicking) is a guitar technique that means you literally pick the strings with your right-hand fingers and thumb. This contrasts with the conventional technique of strumming and playing single notes with a pick (a.k.a. flatpicking). For fingerpicking, you can use any type of guitar: acoustic steel-string, nylon-string classical, or electric.

THE RIGHT HAND

The most common right-hand position is shown here.

Use a high wrist; arch your palm as if you were holding a ping-pong ball. Keep the thumb outside and away from the fingers, and let the fingers do the work rather than lifting your whole hand.

The thumb generally plucks the bottom strings with downstrokes on the left side of the thumb and thumbnail. The other fingers pluck the higher strings using upstokes with the fleshy tip of the fingers and fingernails. The thumb and fingers should pluck one string per stroke and not brush over several strings.

Another picking option you may choose to use is called hybrid picking (a.k.a. plectrum-style fingerpicking). Here, the pick is usually held between the thumb and first finger, and the three remaining fingers are assigned to pluck the higher strings.

THE LEFT HAND

The left-hand fingers are numbered 1 though 4.

Be sure to keep your fingers arched, with each joint bent; if they flatten out across the strings, they will deaden the sound when you fingerpick. As a general rule, let the strings ring as long as possible when playing fingerstyle.

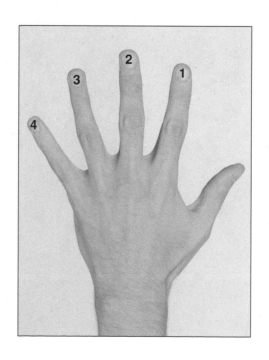

Caravan

from SOPHISTICATED LADIES

Words and Music by Duke Ellington, Irving Mills and Juan Tizol

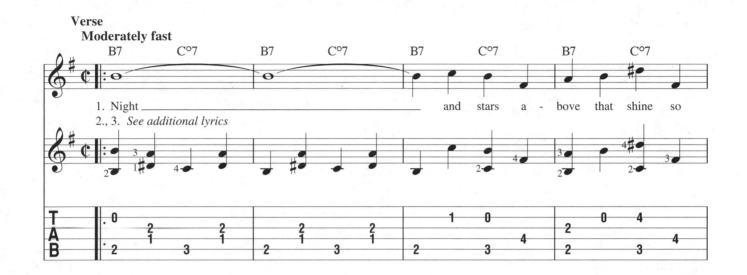

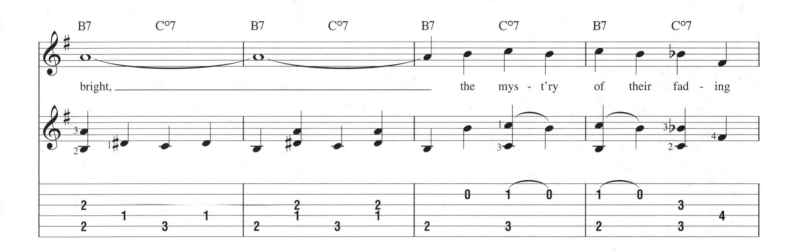

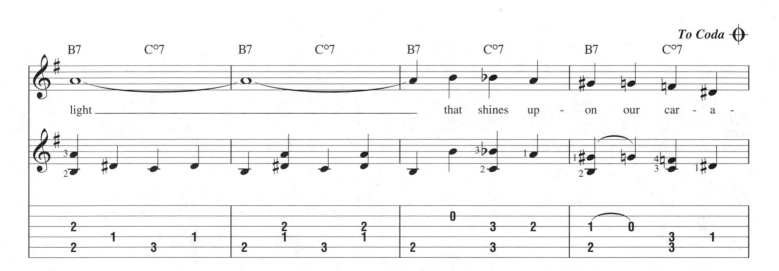

Bridge

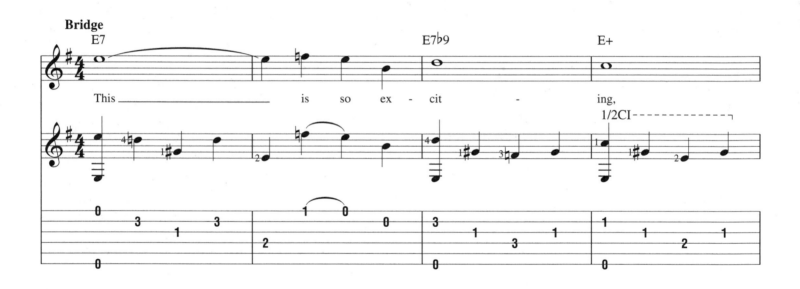

This _____ is so ex - cit - ing,

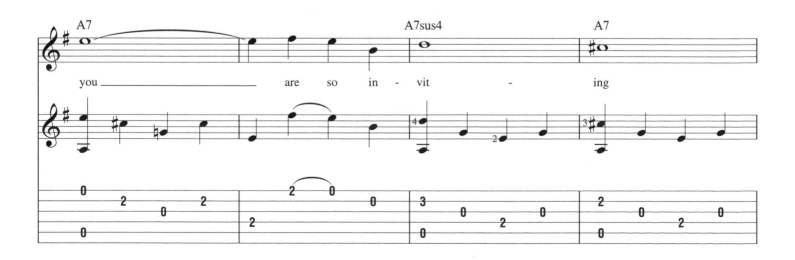

you _____ are so in - vit - ing

rest - ing in my arms as I

D.C. al Coda

thrill to _____ the mag - ic charms _____ of

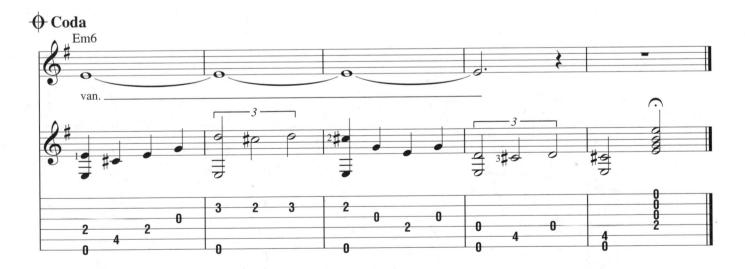

van. _____

Additional Lyrics

2. Sleep upon my shoulder as we creep
Across the sands so I may keep
This memory of our caravan.

3. ...you beside me here beneath the blue.
My dream of love is coming true
Within our desert caravan.

Do Nothin' till You Hear from Me

Words and Music by Duke Ellington and Bob Russell

Drop D tuning:
(low to high) D-A-D-G-B-E

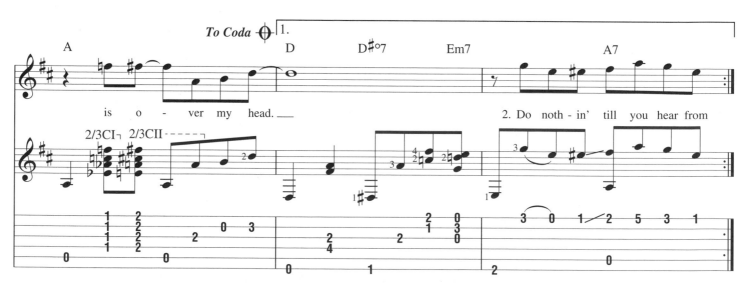

True, I've been seen with some-one new,__ but does that

mean that I'm un - true?__ When we're a - part the words in my heart__ re -

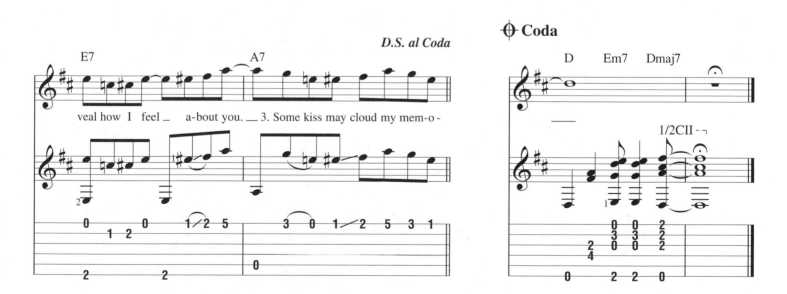

D.S. al Coda

$\oplus$ **Coda**

veal how I feel__ a-bout you.__ 3. Some kiss may cloud my mem-o-

Additional Lyrics

2. Do nothin' till you hear from me.
   At least consider our romance.
   If you should take the word of others you've heard,
   I haven't a chance.

3. Some kiss may cloud my memory
   And other arms may hold a thrill,
   But please do nothin' till you hear it from me
   And you never will.

Don't Get Around Much Anymore

from SOPHISTICATED LADY

Words and Music by Duke Ellington and Bob Russell

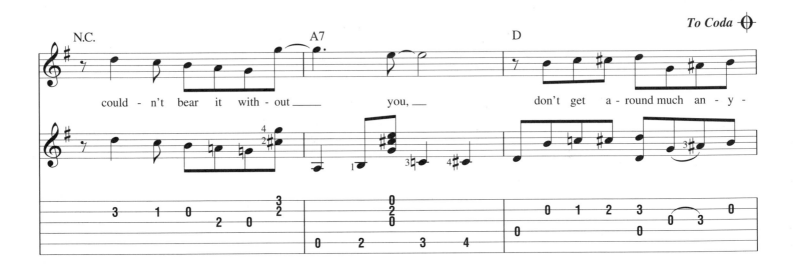

Bridge

Dar - ling, I guess ___ my mind's more at ease, ___ but,

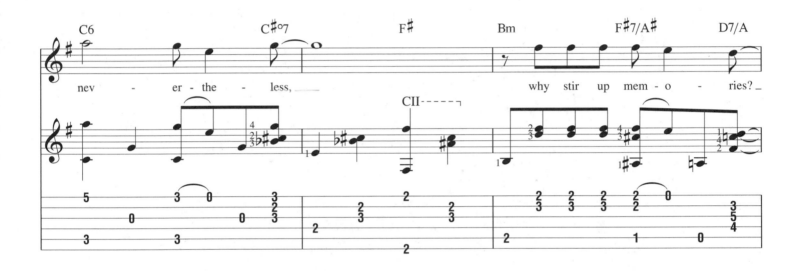

nev - er - the - less, ___ why stir up mem - o - ries? ___

D.S. al Coda

Coda

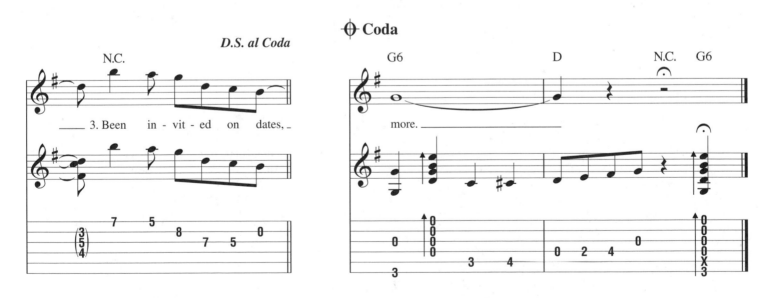

___ 3. Been in - vit - ed on dates, ___

more. ___

Additional Lyrics

2. Thought I'd visit the club,
   Got as far as the door.
   They'd have asked me about you,
   Don't get around much anymore.

3. Been invited on dates,
   Might have gone, but what for?
   Awf'lly diff'rent without you,
   Don't get around much anymore.

I Got It Bad and That Ain't Good

Words by Paul Francis Webster
Music by Duke Ellington

Additional Lyrics

2. My poor heart is sentimental, not made of wood;
   I got it bad and that ain't good!

4. Like a lonely weeping willow lost in the wood;
   I got it bad and that ain't good!

5. And the things I tell my pillow, no woman should;
   I got it bad and that ain't good!

I'm Just a Lucky So and So

Words by Mack David
Music by Duke Ellington

Bridge

ask me the a-mount | in my bank ac-count, | I'd have to con-fess ___ that I'm

slip-pin', ___ but | that don't wor-ry me, | con-fi-den-tial-ly, I've got a

⊕ **Coda**

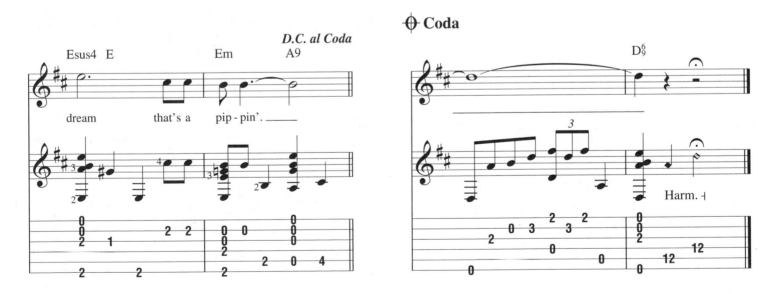

dream | that's a pip-pin'. ___

Additional Lyrics

2. The birds in every tree
Are all so neighborly,
They sing wherever I go.
I guess I'm just a lucky so-and-so.

3. And when the day is through,
Each night I hurry to
A home where love waits, I know.
I guess I'm just a lucky so-and-so.

In a Mellow Tone

Words by Milt Gabler
Music by Duke Ellington

Drop D tuning:
(low to high) D-A-D-G-B-E

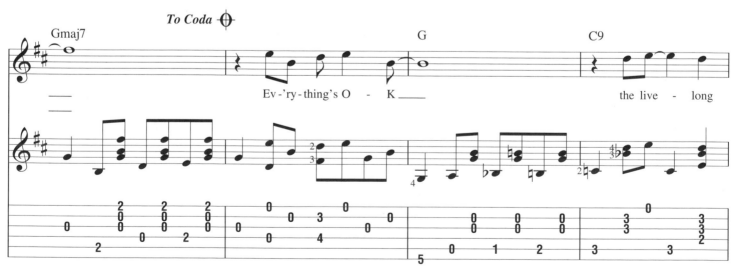

In a Sentimental Mood

Words and Music by Duke Ellington, Irving Mills and Manny Kurtz

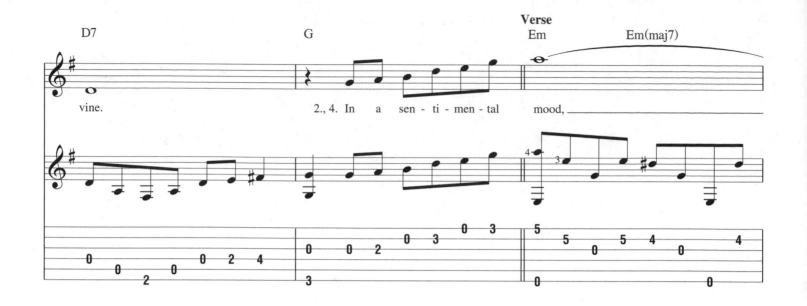

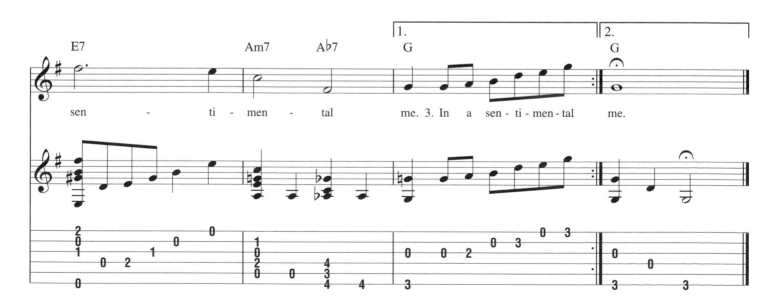

Mood Indigo

from SOPHISTICATED LADIES

Words and Music by Duke Ellington, Irving Mills and Albany Bigard

cares a-bout me, ___ I'm just a soul who's blu-er than blue ___ can be.

When I get that mood in-di-go, ___ I could lay me down and

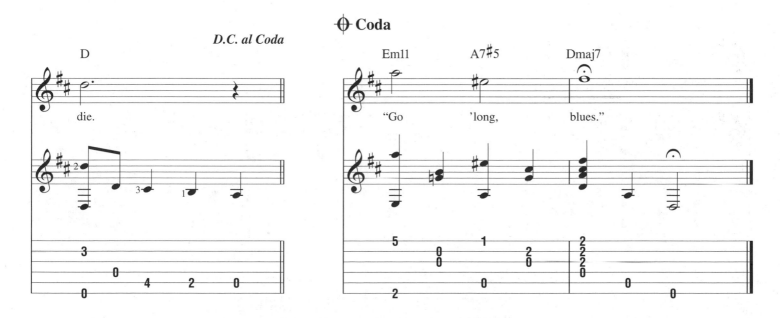

D.C. al Coda

die.

Coda

"Go 'long, blues."

It Don't Mean a Thing
(If It Ain't Got That Swing)

from SOPHISTICATED LADIES

Words and Music by Duke Ellington and Irving Mills

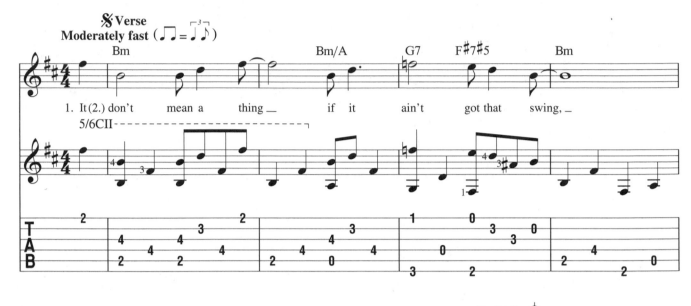

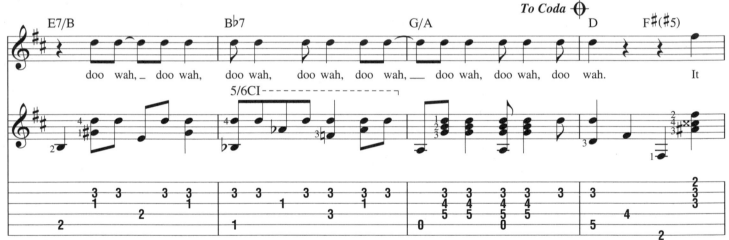

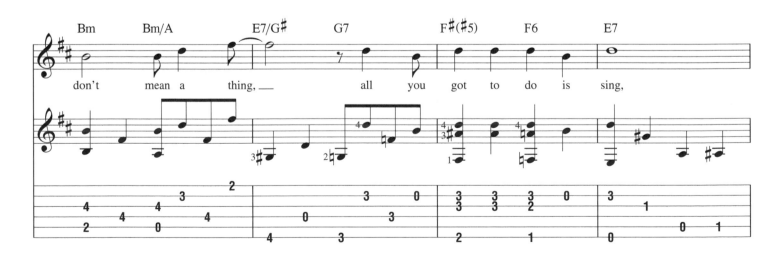

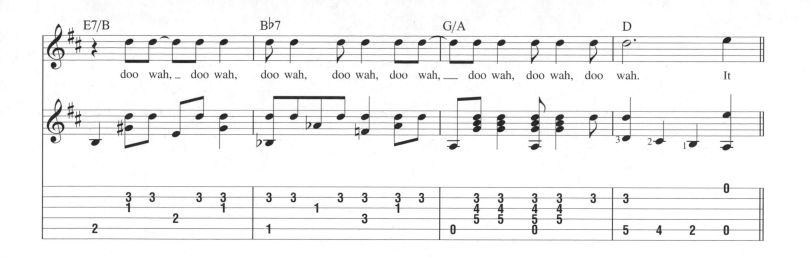

doo wah, ___ doo wah, doo wah, doo wah, doo wah, ___ doo wah, doo wah, doo wah. It

Bridge

makes no dif-f'rence if ___ it's sweet or hot, ___ just give that rhy - thm

D.S. al Coda

ev - 'ry - thing you got. 2. It

Coda

wah.

Perdido

Words by Harry Lenk and Ervin Drake
Music by Juan Tizol

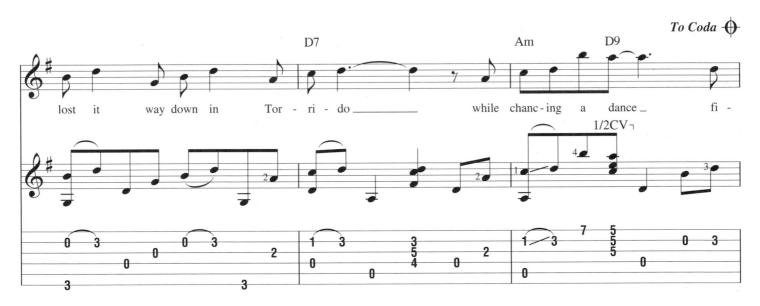

Bridge

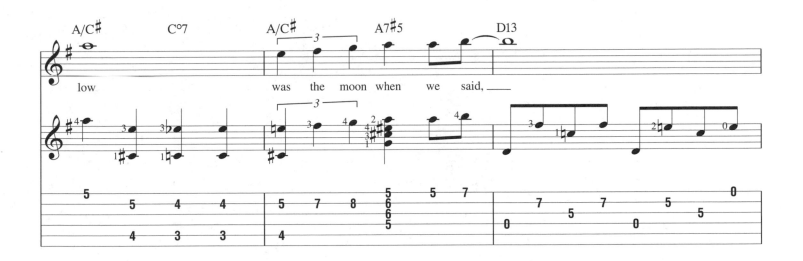

Coda

D.S. al Coda

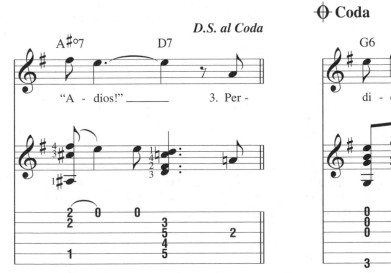

Additional Lyrics

2. Bolero, she glanced as she danced a Bolero.
   I said, taking off my sombrero,
   "Let's meet for a sweet siesta."

3. Perdido, since then has my heart been perdido.
   I know I must go to Torrido;
   That yearning to lose perdido.

Prelude to a Kiss

Words by Irving Gordon and Irving Mills
Music by Duke Ellington

Bridge

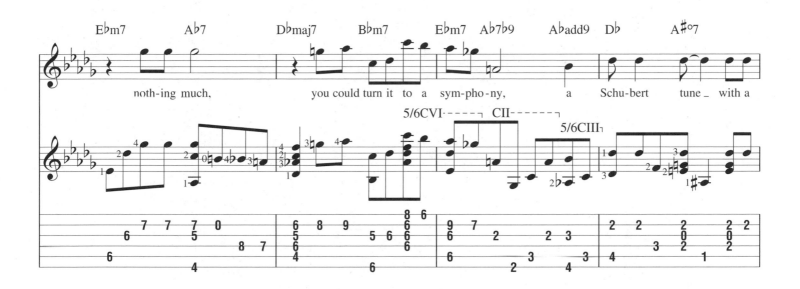

⊕ **Coda**

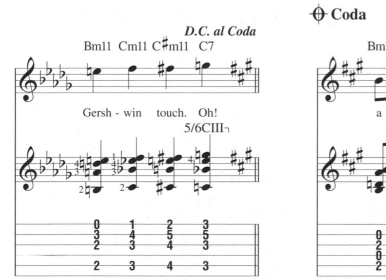

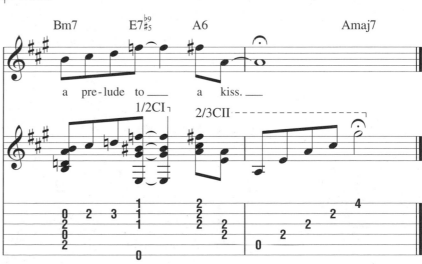

Additional Lyrics

2. If you hear a song that grows
   From my tender sentimental woes,
   That was my heart trying to compose
   A prelude to a kiss.

3. How my love song gently cries
   For the tenderness within your eyes.
   My love is a prelude that never dies,
   A prelude to a kiss.

Satin Doll

from SOPHISTICATED LADIES

Words by Johnny Mercer and Billy Strayhorn
Music by Duke Ellington

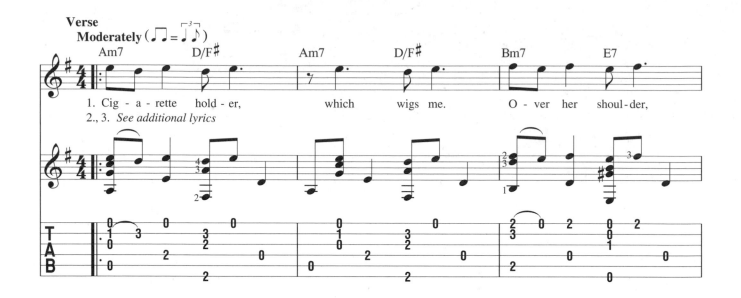

1. Cig - a - rette hold - er, which wigs me. O - ver her shoul - der,
2., 3. *See additional lyrics*

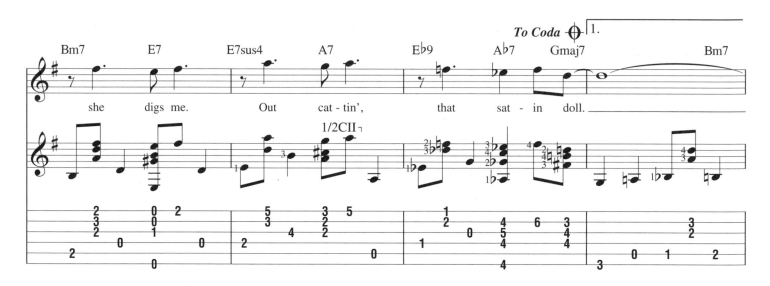

she digs me. Out cat - tin', that sat - in doll. _____

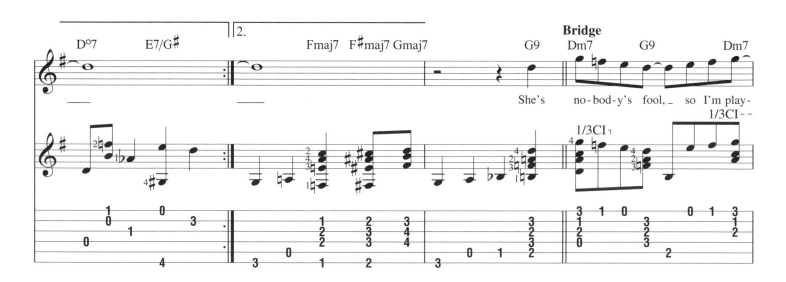

She's no - bod - y's fool, _ so I'm play -

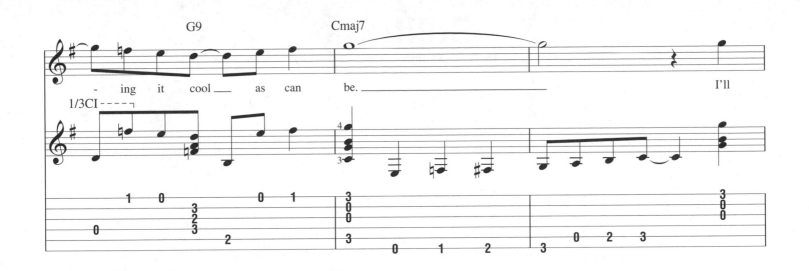

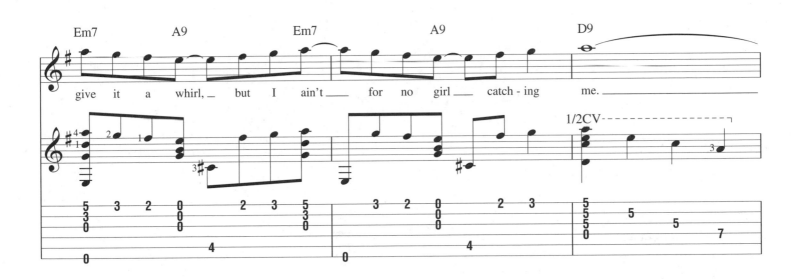

D.C. al Coda

$\oplus$ **Coda**

Additional Lyrics

2. Baby, shall we go out skippin'?
   Careful amigo, you're flippin'.
   Speaks Latin, that satin doll.

3. Telephone numbers, well, you know,
   Doing my rhumbas with uno,
   And that 'n' my satin doll.

Solitude

Words and Music by Duke Ellington, Eddie De Lange and Irving Mills

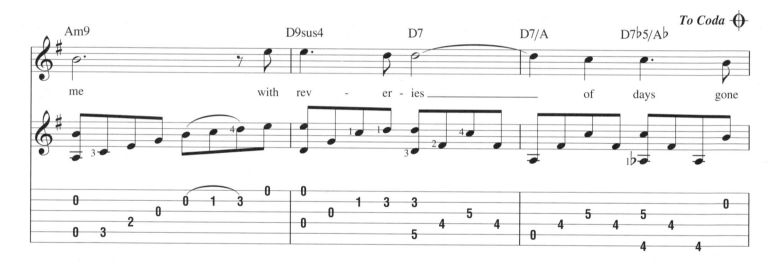

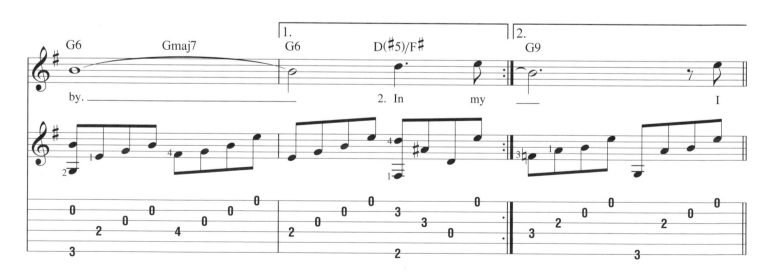

Bridge

sit in my chair, __ I'm filled with de - spair, __ there's no one could be ___ so sad. __

_____ With gloom ev - 'ry - where, __ I sit and I stare; __ I

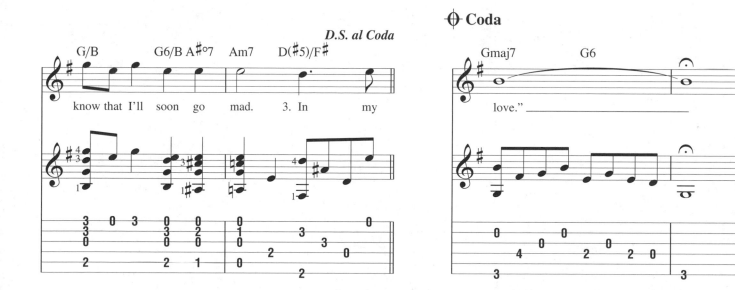

know that I'll soon go mad. 3. In my

love." _____

Additional Lyrics

2. In my solitude, you taunt me
   With memories that never die.

3. In my solitude, I'm praying,
   "Dear Lord above, send back my love."

Sophisticated Lady

from SOPHISTICATED LADIES

Words and Music by Duke Ellington, Irving Mills and Mitchell Parish

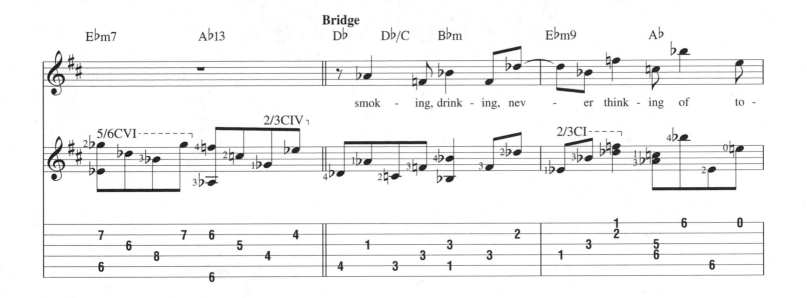

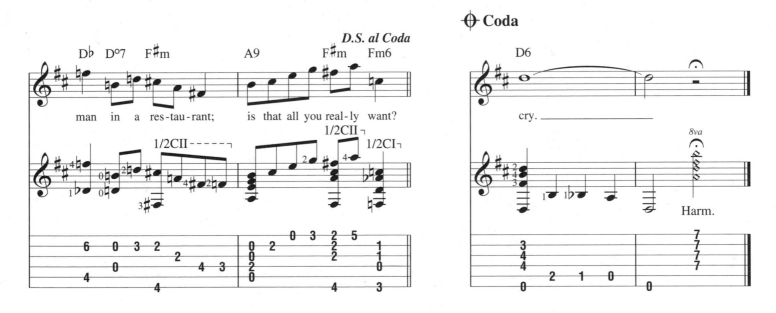

Additional Lyrics

2. Then, with disillusion deep in your eyes,
   You learned that fools in love soon grow wise.
   The years have changed you somehow;
   I see you now...

3. No, sophisticated lady, I know
   You miss the love you lost long ago.
   And when nobody is nigh, you cry.

Take the "A" Train

Words and Music by Billy Strayhorn

Drop D tuning:
(low to high) D-A-D-G-B-E

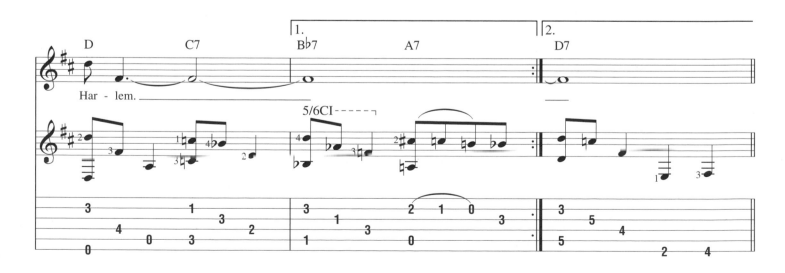

Bridge

Hur - ry! _____ Get on now; it's com - ing! _____

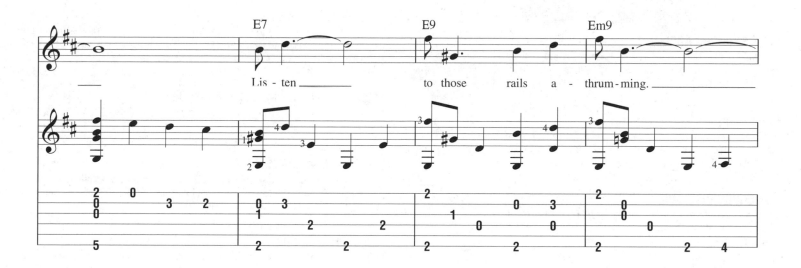

Lis - ten _____ to those rails a - thrum - ming. _____

⊕ Coda

D.C. al Coda

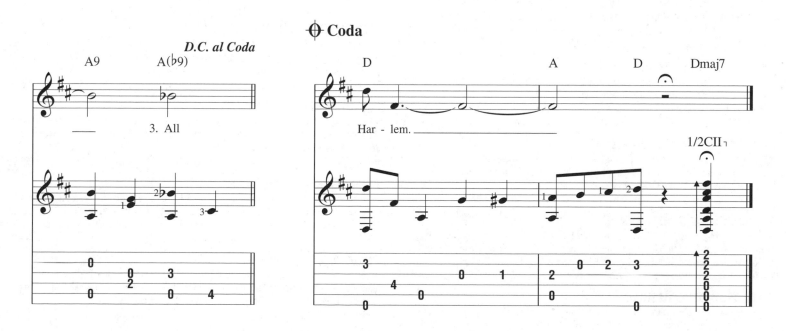

3. All

Har - lem. _____

Additional Lyrics

2. If you miss the "A" train,
You'll find you've missed the quickest way to Harlem.

3. All 'board! Get on the "A" train.
Soon you will be on Sugar Hill in Harlem.

FINGERPICKING
GUITAR BOOKS

Hone your fingerpicking skills with these great songbooks featuring solo guitar arrangements in standard notation and tablature. The arrangements in these books are carefully written for intermediate-level guitarists. Each song combines melody and harmony in one superb guitar fingerpicking arrangement. Each book also includes an introduction to basic fingerstyle guitar.

FINGERPICKING ACOUSTIC
15 songs: Behind Blue Eyes • Best of My Love • Blowin' in the Wind • The Boxer • Dust in the Wind • Helplessly Hoping • Hey Jude • In My Life • Learning to Fly • Leaving on a Jet Plane • Tears in Heaven • Time in a Bottle • You've Got a Friend • and more.
00699614..$9.99

FINGERPICKING ACOUSTIC ROCK
15 songs: American Pie • Bridge over Troubled Water • Every Rose Has Its Thorn • Knockin' on Heaven's Door • Landslide • More Than Words • Norwegian Wood (This Bird Has Flown) • Suite: Judy Blue Eyes • Wanted Dead or Alive • and more.
00699764..$9.99

FINGERPICKING BACH
12 masterpieces from J.S. Bach: Air on the G String • Bourrée in E Minor • Jesu, Joy of Man's Desiring • Little Prelude No. 2 in C Major • Minuet in G • Prelude in C Major • Quia Respexit • Sheep May Safely Graze • and more.
00699793..$8.95

FINGERPICKING BALLADS
15 songs: Against All Odds • (Everything I Do) I Do It for You • Fields of Gold • Have I Told You Lately • It's All Coming Back to Me Now • Looks Like We Made It • Rainy Days and Mondays • Say You, Say Me • She's Got a Way • Your Song • and more.
00699717..$9.99

FINGERPICKING BEATLES
30 songs including: All You Need Is Love • And I Love Her • Can't Buy Me Love • Hey Jude • In My Life • Lady Madonna • Let It Be • Love Me Do • Michelle • Nowhere Man • Please Please Me • Something • Ticket to Ride • Yellow Submarine • Yesterday • and more.
00699049..$19.95

FINGERPICKING CHILDREN'S SONGS
15 songs: Any Dream Will Do • Do-Re-Mi • It's a Small World • Linus and Lucy • The Muppet Show Theme • Puff the Magic Dragon • The Rainbow Connection • Sesame Street Theme • Winnie the Pooh • Zip-A-Dee-Doo-Dah • and more.
00699712..$9.99

FINGERPICKING CHRISTMAS
20 classic carols: Away in a Manger • Deck the Hall • The First Noel • God Rest Ye, Merry Gentlemen • Hark! The Herald Angels Sing • It Came Upon the Midnight Clear • Jingle Bells • O Little Town of Bethlehem • Silent Night • What Child Is This • and more.
00699599..$8.95

FINGERPICKING CLASSICAL
15 songs: Ave Maria • Bourée in E Minor • Canon in D • Eine Kleine Nachtmusik • Für Elise • Habanera • Minuet in G Major (Bach) • Minuet in G Major (Beethoven) • New World Symphony • Pomp and Circumstance • and more.
00699620..$8.95

FINGERPICKING COUNTRY
17 classic favorites: Always on My Mind • By the Time I Get to Phoenix • Could I Have This Dance • Crazy • Green Green Grass of Home • He Stopped Loving Her Today • I Walk the Line • King of the Road • Tennessee Waltz • You Are My Sunshine • and more.
00699687..$9.99

FINGERPICKING DISNEY
15 songs: The Bare Necessities • Beauty and the Beast • Can You Feel the Love Tonight • Colors of the Wind • Go the Distance • If I Didn't Have You • Look Through My Eyes • Reflection • Under the Sea • A Whole New World • You'll Be in My Heart • and more.
00699711..$9.95

FINGERPICKING HYMNS
15 songs: Amazing Grace • Beneath the Cross of Jesus • Come, Thou Fount of Every Blessing • For the Beauty of the Earth • I've Got Peace like a River • Jacob's Ladder • A Mighty Fortress Is Our God • Rock of Ages • and more.
00699688..$8.95

FINGERPICKING ANDREW LLOYD WEBBER
14 songs: All I Ask of You • Don't Cry for Me Argentina • Memory • The Music of the Night • With One Look • more.
00699839..$9.99

FINGERPICKING MOZART
15 of Mozart's timeless compositions: Ave Verum • Eine Kleine Nachtmusik • Laudate Dominum • Minuet in G Major, K. 1 • Piano Concerto No. 21 in C Major • Piano Sonata in A • Piano Sonata in C • Rondo in C Major • and more.
00699794..$8.95

FINGERPICKING POP
Includes 15 songs: Can You Feel the Love Tonight • Don't Know Why • Endless Love • Imagine • Let It Be • My Cherie Amour • My Heart Will Go On • Piano Man • Stand by Me • We've Only Just Begun • Wonderful Tonight • and more.
00699615..$9.99

FINGERPICKING PRAISE
15 songs: Above All • Breathe • Draw Me Close • Great Is the Lord • He Is Exalted • Jesus, Name Above All Names • Oh Lord, You're Beautiful • Open the Eyes of My Heart • Shine, Jesus, Shine • Shout to the Lord • You Are My King • and more.
00699714..$8.95

FINGERPICKING ROCK
15 songs: Abracadabra • Brown Eyed Girl • Crocodile Rock • Free Bird • The House of the Rising Sun • I Want You to Want Me • Livin' on a Prayer • Maggie May • Rhiannon • Still the Same • When the Children Cry • and more.
00699716..$9.99

FINGERPICKING STANDARDS
17 fantastic songs: Can't Help Falling in Love • Fly Me to the Moon • Georgia on My Mind • I Just Called to Say I Love You • Just the Way You Are • Misty • Moon River • Unchained Melody • What a Wonderful World • When I Fall in Love • Yesterday • and more.
00699613..$9.99

FINGERPICKING WEDDING
15 tunes for the big day: Beautiful in My Eyes • Don't Know Much • Endless Love • Grow Old with Me • In My Life • The Lord's Prayer • This Is the Day (A Wedding Song) • We've Only Just Begun • Wedding Processional • You and I • and more.
00699637..$9.99

FINGERPICKING YULETIDE
16 holiday favorites: Blue Christmas • The Christmas Song • Frosty the Snow Man • A Holly Jolly Christmas • I'll Be Home for Christmas • Jingle-Bell Rock • Let It Snow! Let It Snow! Let It Snow! • Merry Christmas, Darling • Rudolph the Red-Nosed Reindeer • and more.
00699654..$9.99

FOR MORE INFORMATION, SEE YOUR LOCAL MUSIC DEALER, OR WRITE TO:

HAL•LEONARD®
CORPORATION

7777 W. BLUEMOUND RD. P.O. BOX 13819 MILWAUKEE, WI 53213

Visit Hal Leonard online at **www.halleonard.com**

Prices, contents and availability subject to change without notice.

PLAY THE CLASSICS
JAZZ FOLIOS FOR GUITARISTS

BEST OF JAZZ GUITAR
by Wolf Marshall • Signature Licks INCLUDES TAB

In this book/CD pack, Wolf Marshall provides a hands-on analysis of 10 of the most frequently played tunes in the jazz genre, as played by the leading guitarists of all time. Features: All the Things You Are • How Insensitive • I'll Remember April • So What • Yesterdays • and more.
00695586 Book/CD Pack......................................$24.95

GUITAR STANDARDS
Classic Jazz Masters Series INCLUDES TAB

16 classic jazz guitar performances transcribed note for note with tablature: All of You (Kenny Burrell) • Easter Parade (Herb Ellis) • I'll Remember April (Grant Green) • Lover Man (Django Reinhardt) • Song for My Father (George Benson) • The Way You Look Tonight (Wes Montgomery) • and more. Includes a discography.
00699143 Guitar Transcriptions $14.95

JAZZ CLASSICS
Jazz Guitar Chord Melody Solos
arr. Jeff Arnold INCLUDES TAB

27 rich arrangements of jazz classics: Blue in Green • Bluesette • Doxy • Epistrophy • Footprints • Giant Steps • Lush Life • A Night in Tunisia • Nuages • St. Thomas • Waltz for Debby • Yardbird Suite • and more.
00699758 Solo Guitar $12.95

JAZZ CLASSICS FOR SOLO GUITAR
arranged by Robert B. Yelin INCLUDES TAB

This collection includes excellent chord melody arrangements in standard notation and tablature for 35 all-time jazz favorites: April in Paris • Cry Me a River • Day by Day • God Bless' the Child • It Might as Well Be Spring • Lover • My Romance • Nuages • Satin Doll • Tenderly • Unchained Melody • Wave • and more!
00699279 Solo Guitar $17.95

JAZZ FAVORITES FOR SOLO GUITAR
arranged by Robert B. Yelin INCLUDES TAB

This fantastic 35-song collection includes lush chord melody arrangements in standard notation and tab: Autumn in New York • Call Me Irresponsible • How Deep Is the Ocean • I Could Write a Book • The Lady Is a Tramp • Mood Indigo • Polka Dots and Moonbeams • Solitude • Take the "A" Train • Where or When • more.
00699278 Solo Guitar $17.95

JAZZ FOR THE ROCK GUITARIST
by Michael Mueller INCLUDES TAB

Take your playing beyond barre chords and the blues box! This book/CD pack will take you through the essentials of the jazz idiom with plenty of exercises and examples – all of which are demonstrated on the accompanying CD.
00695856 Book/CD Pack......................................$14.95

JAZZ GEMS FOR SOLO GUITAR
arranged by Robert B. Yelin INCLUDES TAB

35 great solo arrangements of jazz classics, including: After You've Gone • Alice in Wonderland • The Christmas Song • Four • Meditation • Stompin' at the Savoy • Sweet and Lovely • Waltz for Debby • Yardbird Suite • You'll Never Walk Alone • You've Changed • and more.
00699617 Solo Guitar $17.95

JAZZ GUITAR BIBLE
INCLUDES TAB

The one book that has all of the jazz guitar classics transcribed note-for-note, with standard notation and tablature. Includes over 30 songs: Body and Soul • Girl Talk • I'll Remember April • In a Sentimental Mood • My Funny Valentine • Nuages • Satin Doll • So What • Stardust • Take Five • Tangerine • Yardbird Suite • and more.
00690466 Guitar Recorded Versions $19.95

JAZZ GUITAR CHORD MELODIES
arranged & performed by Dan Towey INCLUDES TAB

This book/CD pack includes complete solo performances of 12 standards, including: All the Things You Are • Body and Soul • My Romance • How Insensitive • My One and Only Love • and more. The arrangements are performance level and range in difficulty from intermediate to advanced.
00698988 Book/CD Pack $19.95

JAZZ GUITAR PLAY-ALONG
Guitar Play-Along Volume 16 INCLUDES TAB

With this book/CD pack, all you have to do is follow the tab, listen to the CD to hear how the guitar should sound, and then play along using the separate backing tracks. 8 songs: All Blues • Bluesette • Footprints • How Insensitive (Insensatez) • Misty • Satin Doll • Stella by Starlight • Tenor Madness.
00699584 Book/CD Pack $15.95

JAZZ STANDARDS FOR FINGERSTYLE GUITAR
INCLUDES TAB

20 songs, including: All the Things You Are • Autumn Leaves • Bluesette • Body and Soul • Fly Me to the Moon • The Girl from Ipanema • How Insensitive • I've Grown Accustomed to Her Face • My Funny Valentine • Satin Doll • Stompin' at the Savoy • and more.
00699029 Fingerstyle Guitar $10.95

JAZZ STANDARDS FOR SOLO GUITAR
arranged by Robert B. Yelin INCLUDES TAB

35 chord melody guitar arrangements, including: Ain't Misbehavin' • Autumn Leaves • Bewitched • Cherokee • Darn That Dream • Girl Talk • I've Got You Under My Skin • Lullaby of Birdland • My Funny Valentine • A Nightingale Sang in Berkeley Square • Stella by Starlight • The Very Thought of You • and more.
00699277 Solo Guitar $17.95

101 MUST-KNOW JAZZ LICKS
by Wolf Marshall

Add a jazz feel and flavor to your playing! 101 definitive licks, plus a demonstration CD, from every major jazz guitar style, neatly organized into easy-to-use categories. They're all here: swing and pre-bop, bebop, post-bop modern jazz, hard bop and cool jazz, modal jazz, soul jazz and postmodern jazz.
00695433 Book/CD Pack.....................................$17.95

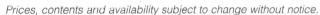

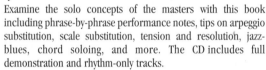